How to Find Morels

How to Find Morels

TEXT AND PHOTOGRAPHY
Milan Pelouch

RECIPES BY
Lila Pelouch

THE UNIVERSITY OF MICHIGAN PRESS
Ann Arbor

2017   2016   2015   2014   5   4   3   2

A CIP catalog record for this book is available from the British Library.

Library of Congress Cataloging-in-Publication Data

Pelouch, Milan, 1930–
    How to find morels / text and photography,
Milan Pelouch ; recipes by Lila Pelouch.
        p.   cm.
    ISBN-13: 978-0-472-03274-7 (pbk. : alk. paper)
    ISBN-10: 0-472-03274-7 (pbk. : alk. paper)
    1. Morels.   2. Cookery (Morels)   I. Title.

QK623.M65P45   2008
641.3'58—dc22   2007035437

Most authors dedicate their work to their family, the wife, husband, children, and grandchildren. I feel that my family has been amply gratified by sharing with me some of my insatiable quest to chase after the elusive creature of the forest—the mushroom—covering hundreds of square miles of the continent, as well as sharing the pleasure of consuming the quarry.

Instead, I dedicate this book to all who share my love of nature for what it offers in terms of beauty to those willing to open their eyes and for the fruits it provides to all willing to learn, explore, and gather its largesse.

My first steps hunting mushrooms were in the company and under the guidance of my grandfather. Love of this pastime and appreciation of the knowledge I gained from him have enriched all my days since then. I wish to impart the same enjoyment to all willing to take the book, put on a pair of boots, and enter the natural world in which fungi have such an important role.

Mushroom hunting is a truly rewarding pursuit with many dimensions. It provides more physical exercise than golf or fishing and rewards the hunter with something that is healthy and savory on the physical side and a sense of achievement in the game of hide-and-seek on the phrenic, spiritual side.

The novice I urge to take the first steps to learn. Those who have already made a beginning and seek to improve their rate of success I urge to read my book and continue their endeavors. And to all I wish the enjoyment that comes with accomplishment.

Contents

Introduction

Some 2,000 or more years ago, people searched for mushrooms in order to enhance their diet. Although much has changed over the centuries in the human diet, hunting wild mushrooms continues to hold interest for many people, be it as food for the dining room table or as a fun and healthy hobby.

There are many kinds of mushrooms that serve both purposes; on this continent, the one that stands out above the rest is the morel. There is something exciting, almost magical, about this fragile fungus that weighs barely an ounce.

First of all, morels are unlike other mushrooms in appearance and in their exotic, woodsy taste. Perhaps morels are even more prized because it is challenging to find them. They appear without warning at different times, their life span is relatively short, they are well camouflaged to escape a hunter's searching eye, and the locations where they appear can seem unpredictable to both a beginning and an accomplished mushroom hunter.

Over the years I have run into many frustrated morel hunters. I can well sympathize with their disappointments since, before I became addicted to the pursuit of hunting wild mushrooms, I ended many a day of scrambling up steep hills without having much to show for it. That is understandable. Morels are tricky creatures. Nature gave them the same talents it gave to the chameleon and the octopus: they can blend into the environment so well that only a hunter with a trained, sharp eye, intense concentration, and thorough knowledge of their habitat and behavior can discover their hiding places.

More than a few times have I spotted a morel just poking its head from under the leaf cover only to lose sight of it. The moment I see one I freeze and scrutinize the whole area because where there is one there are often others and it is easy to step on the better hidden ones. Looking around and poking likely hiding places with my stick, I usually soon discover another specimen and perhaps a third one or even more. I bend down, open my knife, harvest my first mushroom, deposit it into my canvas bag, and, feeling satisfied, look for the beauty I saw a minute before. Only it's not there any more. Like a clever little creature it realized it was in mortal danger and ducked someplace out of view. The best thing to do at this point is to step back to the original location and look for the spot where you first saw the mushroom because often a hiding morel can only be seen from a certain angle. Sometimes it takes several minutes to rediscover the mushroom despite the fact that I mentally marked its location when I first saw it. That's how well these treasures of Mother Nature can hide. So it's no wonder that a novice has a hard time filling his or her bag. Especially if he or she doesn't have a clue where to look.

So one can understand the frustration of coming back empty-handed. That devastating feeling can lead some aspiring morel hunters to try cloak and dagger games. They probably walked by quite a few mushrooms, but they blame their failure on not knowing the "spots." The solution, they think, is to do a little spying on some of the more successful mushroomers.

Most mushroom hunters don't stay in expensive motels while on a hunt. They usually stay in their recreational vehicle in a campground or pitch a tent in a state forest in reasonable proximity to their hunting grounds. And if one has suffered through several unsuccessful expeditions and is tired of walking around all day and having nothing to show for it, one may succumb to the temptation to spy on some of the "lucky" confreres. He or she sees certain individuals in the campground cleaning a handsome pile of mushrooms, and the frustration grows.

Usually the best place to gather some meaningful intelligence on the subject is the campground latrine. The bathroom in the morning is like a Reuters agency—it buzzes with all sorts of reports on the best places to look for mushrooms. Of course one has to distinguish between the true accounts, which are usually in short supply, and propaganda designed to deceive and throw the competition off track. If a fellow in pajama pants covered with pictures of fly agarics claims he picked a couple of bushel baskets full of morels in half an hour about 50 miles farther north, and if he is willing to share the coordinates of his discovery, the recipient of the report should know that this could be information of dubious value.

Similarly, you cannot trust a guy who is trying to convince everybody that it is a waste of time to hunt and this is the poorest season in half a century and a waste of effort, especially when his hands are heavily stained with morel juice. If there are no promising leads from these reports, many unsuccessful mushroomers resort to more aggressive methods to gain the required information on the hot hunting areas. Some select a centrally located spot in the campground, preferably one blessed with good acoustics, wait until afternoon when the mushroom hunters are coming home from the woods, and then sit tight watching for signs of mushroom success. And when they firmly establish that the fellow on site 22 has been cleaning his or her haul longer than anyone else, they simply jot down that person's license plate number and get ready to play detective. Next morning they'll be waiting by the campground exit with their engines running and their Global Positioning System (GPS) units turned on. When the successful hunter emerges they follow.

Of course, an experienced morel hunter guards his or her secret locations. The wily hunter has a clean rearview mirror and, having spotted a suspicious vehicle, takes appropriate countermeasures to lose the tracking spy. I once made the mistake of dumping two baskets of *Morchella esculenta* on a picnic table in broad daylight. Next morning a procession of several cars followed me as I was leaving the campground. I turned my headlights on and slowly led them straight into the local cemetery.

Other people are more direct. They try to secure the necessary information by direct interrogation. They casually walk by your picnic table stacked with the aromatic treasure and just as casually ask, "My, where did you find those good-looking mushrooms?" And, as the saying goes, if you are foolish enough to ask the question, you're foolish enough to believe the answer, for a dedicated, successful morel hunter will take the secret of his or her "mushroom spots" to the grave.

But there is no need to spy on other mushroom hunters. The best policy is to find mushrooms the old-fashioned way—work at it. Anybody with decent eyesight, leg joints free of arthritis, an ability to scale some fairly hilly terrain, the necessary knowledge of what the quarry looks like—that is a few rules of thumb about their habitat—and a bit of patience can find morels if they are in season and growing.

It is the goal of this book to give the reader the best insight into knowledge about the best places to find morels. The following chapters will show you what to pick and what to leave for the critters, which tools you will need for a successful foray, how to zero in on a promising area, how to locate the well-concealed quarry, which is invisible to so many eyes, and what to do once you manage to fill a sack with them. It will also tell you how to make sure you emerge out of the woods in the neighborhood of the place you used for entry! It's all here. All you need, as a football coach would say, is execution . . .

These chapters will give you a running start, your proficiency will increase with experience, and, while doing it, you will have fun and get a better physical workout than pumping iron in an expensive fitness center or health club—and be rewarded for it with a delicious, healthy meal. So, let's curl up on a couch, put a pillow under the rump, and get started! It will pay off when we step among the trees!

Know Thy Quarry!

Unlike mycology in general, in which the species and often even the genus of a mushroom can be difficult to identify—making it hazardous for a novice to collect mushrooms for culinary purposes since a number of species are toxic and a few are even deadly poisonous—the few species of edible morels are relatively easy to identify. With some knowledge and a little care and caution, one does not have to fear getting sick. Of course, a few precautions must be taken even with the easily identifiable morels. For instance, it is not recommended that any species of the morel family be eaten raw. There are also individuals who are allergic to fungi in general and morels in particular. When you partake of these delicious fruits of the forest for the first time, limit the quantity you ingest to an "experimental amount," that is, just a few mouthfuls. There will be more about cooking and eating morels in a later chapter. Now let's get acquainted with the more common members of the family!

Morchellaceae, the True Morels

The Black Morel

Morchella angusticeps
The black morel is very easy to recognize. The adjective *black* is really a misnomer because the head is not truly black but

rather dark brown, grayish-brown, or even dark tan. In a full-grown mushroom the head is about 2 to 4 inches long, conical in shape, and composed of pits or ridges of irregular shape and pattern. The head is firmly attached to the top of the stem (the stalk or leg, what mycologists call the stipe), without an overhang, and the stem is whitish or creamy white. The entire mushroom is hollow, including the stem, which contains no cottonlike substance and is typically ½ to ¾ inch in diameter. When viewed closely, it may be decorated with tiny iridescent particles. The top of the head is usually rounded but sometimes pointed. While the normal shape of the head is elongated, we sometimes see a quasi-spherical shape. The outer surface of the ridges is darker than the inner

A typical black morel, *Morchella angusticeps*

valleys. The body is usually more "meaty" than that of a related species, *Morchella conica*.

Black morels usually appear as single mushrooms, sometimes as twins, rarely as triplets, and never in large clusters.

Morchella conica

Morchella conica is very similar to the *angusticeps*, except, as its scientific name implies, the head is more pointed. The stem is also longer in relation to the head, which is often quite short (1½ to 2½ inches), the body is usually not as meaty, and the stem is thinner and more fragile. This species is lumped together with *Morchella angusticeps* in some guides, but there are some differences, albeit small. Because of the meatiness of the *angusticeps*, I prefer it for the kitchen table.

The Half-Free Morel

Morchella semilibera

The principal difference between the half-free and the more common black morel is that the cap of the half-free variety is attached to the stem down to approximately one-half of the head height, forming a partial overhang of the stem.

The head is typically lighter in color, olive brown or light tan, and substantially shorter, usually only 1 inch or so in length. On the other hand, the stem is longer, hollow, and colored much like that of the black morel. Once again there is no cottony material inside the hollow stem.

The ridges on the cap often tend to be vertical with horizontal separations as opposed to the random patterns found on other morels. The stem is sometimes swollen at the bottom and becomes furrowed with age. The half-free morel is rarer than the black, and, because of the smaller size of the cap, less desirable to cooks.

It is also similar to another species, *Verpa bohemica*, which

Half-free morel, *Morchella semilibera*

is discussed later. As opposed to the black, the half-free morel is commonly found as twins or triplets. Clusters of more than three bodies are extremely rare.

The Gray Morel

Morchella deliciosa

Several species of morels usually make their appearance sequentially in the spring. The black morels peek out first, followed by the grays and then the yellows. Some overlapping does take place depending on the weather. The shape of the gray morel's body is often similar to that of the black morel, although the head is usually a bit heftier than that of the slender blacks. The color of the head is substantially lighter, as the name implies, usually grayish-tan or distinctly gray as in the photos below. The pits or ridges are quite deep, the length of the body of a mature mushroom is roughly 3 to 5 inches, and the length of the stem often approaches one-third of the total length of the body. The entire body is hollow, including the stem, which is also whitish or creamy white with no material present inside. The body is usually thicker or more meaty than that of a black morel, and the scent is less pungent. In the kitchen there is no distinction between the gray and its yellow cousin.

As opposed to the black and half-free morels, the grays often pop up in whole clusters; sometimes more than a dozen individual bodies are connected at the ground level, although,

A couple of specimens of gray morels, *Morchella deliciosa*

as is evident in the photos, single specimens are also found and, in fact, are found more often.

While taxonomists usually designate the gray as a separate species, some mycologists believe it is only an early variant of the yellow morel, *Morchella esculenta*. I tend to agree with these mycologists since I sometimes find a cluster of baby grays and leave them to grow a bit, and when I return they are buff in color. Thus, one might reach the conclusion that this species of morel appears first as a light-grayish mushroom while later assuming a more creamy yellow coloring. However, I am not a professional mycologist, nor do I conduct exhaustive studies of the subtle differences between the spores of the two species or other subtle criteria that can help differentiate between them.

The Yellow Morel

Morchella esculenta

The yellow morel is in many aspects quite similar to its gray sibling. Its principal distinguishing feature is the color of the

A yellow morel, *Morchella esculenta*

Another specimen of *Morchella esculenta*

cap, which is distinctly more ocherous—yellow to creamy yellow—when mature.

Once again, the cap is solidly joined to the stem without a free, overhanging skirt. The pits are deep, the separating ridges are somewhat thinner, and the cap is more elongated. (When young, both the gray morel and the yellow are more elliptical; the cap on the yellow later grows somewhat more conical). The shape of the head is rarely quasi-spherical.

The yellow morel, like its gray cousin, is meatier than the black morel; hence, many mycophagists prefer it. As is the case with the gray morel, the yellow sometimes appears singly but is more often found in scattered groups or even clusters of as many as a dozen or more. In northern Michigan the *esculenta*, under normal weather conditions, appears around the second week of May. At the end of May, sometimes as late as a week or two after Memorial Day, they grow to a very large size with some specimens reaching a length of over 8 inches.

Some folks consider these giant morels to be a separate species of the genus *Morchella*. I personally think, once again,

A cluster of *Morchella esculenta*

that they are a late variant of the *esculenta* because they are almost identical to the earlier, smaller version of the mushroom in all aspects except size.

The False Morels

The Cap

Verpa bohemica

Verpa bohemica, while in some ways resembling a true morel, has several distinguishing features. First, the cap is attached to the stem only at the very top of the stem, forming a loose, overhanging skirt. The attachment is localized, and hence very fragile, so it is very easy to separate the mushroom head from the stem. This is not the case with true morels.

Second, while the stem is hollow, it is filled with a cottony substance. The cap has a series of ridges, but the valleys between the ridges are not as deep as those found in true morels. The shape of the cap is conical to campanulate, and the color tends to be yellowish-brown when there is sufficient moisture but turns a darker brown when dry.

Two specimens of *Verpa bohemica*, moist and dry

While they are considered edible in small quantities (indeed, many pickers collect them, especially when true morels are scarce), there is some danger associated with the ingestion of this mushroom (more about edibility later). When they are picked for eating, only the cap is used. The cottony stem is always discarded. *Verpa bohemica* is generally found in the same habitat as the true morels, but it prefers moist to wet soil. In the absence of adequate moisture the cap dries out rapidly.

Verpa conica
Verpa conica is in some respects similar to *bohemica*; however, the cap is smoother, with a noticeable absence of deep ridges,

Verpa conica

and more campanulate (somewhat resembling the shape of a particular type of ladies' hat). It is brown to yellowish-brown and attached to the stem only marginally at the very top, an attachment sometimes described as free.

The flesh is waxy and quite fragile, and the stem tends to be creamy yellow as opposed to the pure white of most true morels. It is hollow. *Verpa conica* is one of the first mushrooms to appear in the woods in the spring, often before most morel hunters venture out; thus, it is not found very often and is considered rather rare. *Verpa conica* is considered edible, although, due to its scarcity, it is not often used in the kitchen.

The Beefsteak Morel

Gyromitra esculenta

Gyromitra are false morels, although they differ significantly not only from the true morels but even from the *Verpas*. The body of *Gyromitra esculenta* is usually about 3 to 5 inches high, is appreciably heftier and wider, has irregular wrinklelike ridges, and is usually light to dark brown.

Gyromitra esculenta

It is enlarged at the base so that its stem does not at all resemble that of true morels or *Verpa*. The stem is typically quite massive and often almost hidden by the large head. The head is sometimes concave to deeply saddle-shaped. Although *Gyromitra* are considered edible in Europe, the North American variety can be highly toxic and should be avoided. I will discuss the edibility of the entire genus in a later chapter.

Gyromitra caroliniana

As opposed to *Gyromitra esculenta*, the head of the *caroliniana* is more tightly wrinkled, and the stem is not as enlarged—more closely resembling the stem of a true morel, though heftier.

The flesh is solid, white, and has a pleasant scent. Although more prevalent in the Southeast, as the name implies, I have found several specimens as far north as central Missouri. As opposed to the *esculenta*, it is considered edible; however, because of the possibility of confusing it with several other species of toxic *Gyromitra*, it is not recommended that beginners collect it for consumption.

This species of *Gyromitra* is the closest in appearance to the true morels, although a close examination of the ridged and heftier stem and the size and color of the head should provide sufficient clues to its true identity.

Gyromitra caroliniana

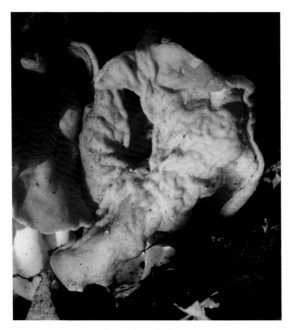

Gyromitra fastigiata

Gyromitra fastigiata

This species of *Gyromitra* usually appears later in the season than the others. The cap is sometimes saddle-shaped, at times resembling an elephant's ear with varicose veins extending over the smooth surface. It is usually reddish-brown but sometimes light brown. Some taxonomists do not classify it as a *Gyromitra* at all, placing it in the genus *Helvella* (specifically *Helvella underwoodii*). In many respects it resembles *Helvella* more than *Gyromitra*.

There are other species of *Gyromitra*, but since this volume is not a field guide or encyclopedia of spring mushrooms, this discussion is confined to the most common species of true and false morels—at least those a novice is likely to encounter in pursuit of the edible varieties.

Fortunately, it is difficult to confuse the true morels with their false cousins. Even the most similar variety, *Verpa bohemica*, can be readily identified on close examination.

As we shall see, some morels live in a symbiotic relationship with certain trees. What this means is that the fungus's mycelia and the tree develop a "give-and-take" relationship, which mycologists call "mycorrhizal," in which the mycelia envelop the tree's roots and penetrate the root covering. The relationship is not parasitic; rather it is a system of mutually agreeable exchange in which the tree supplies certain nutrients to the fungus and vice versa. Each species is quite selective when it comes to its partner, and this affinity comes in handy when we look for small, hard-to-spot mushrooms. By zeroing in on easy-to-spot trees, we are more likely to locate the hiding places of the mushrooms. Once we know which kinds of trees provide sanctuary to the mushroom species we are looking for, our job of hunting them becomes a whole lot easier. Many experienced mushroom hunters possess this knowledge; only a few are willing to share it. It is the goal of this volume to reveal the secrets that will enable the novice to be as successful at this healthy and enjoyable pursuit as experienced old hands. In less than an hour you can gain the needed know-how and will be flashing a big smile on the way home from a successful hunt instead of stewing in frustration after being skunked once again.

Handy Implements of a Mushroom Hunter

Hunting mushrooms is an outdoor activity often conducted in inclement weather. You might wonder what to wear when hunting morels. If you go out fairly early in the morning—which can be a bit cool, especially in northern climates—you will want to dress in layers. As the day warms up and blood starts circulating because of the exertion of going up and down steep hills, you can put the unneeded sweater or sweatshirt into a day pack. Carry a folded raincoat in the backpack as well, just in case.

By far the most important part of a mushroomer's attire is sturdy footwear. I recommend a pair of light hiking boots, preferably with a waterproof lining and certainly with a good ridged sole for traction. It is important to have good ankle support because one typically traverses rough terrain. Good boots not only keep your feet dry when the vegetation is wet from a night rain or early morning condensation, but they also help prevent a twisted ankle and help steady your balance in the hilly terrain where morels are typically found. In fact, I add waterproof gaiters since wet vegetation on the forest floor requires that legs be protected up to the knees. If your feet are wet and cold, the rest of your body will not be comfortable.

With the hilly terrain and the host of obstacles you might encounter, it is a good idea to carry a walking stick. My preference is for one cut from striped maple, which is very light yet quite sturdy. Not only can the stick save you from a fall, but it can also allow you to lift vegetation without having to bend down. You can use it to tap suspicious bumps that are often a sign of a flush of young mushrooms pushing their way up through the surface.

My day pack contains other items besides a raincoat—including my camera and, more important, a quart of drinking water. The water is a must-take item since one tends to perspire and, thus, is in danger of dehydration just a few hours into the hunt, even if it is not a particularly warm day.

In my flannel or woolen shirt pocket I always carry a small bottle of mosquito repellent. This is the time of the year when bugs are waking up, and a good repellent not only can save you from mosquito bites but is also a credible defense against ticks. Ticks are not usually a problem in the upper Midwest this early in the year, but they can be a nuisance a little later and in other parts of the country where they can be transmitters of serious diseases.

Bug repellents come with a wide variety of ingredients and concentrations. The most common formula uses DEET (di-ethyl-toluamide), ranging from concentrations of just a few percent to almost 100 percent of the active ingredient. I always reach for a formula containing at least 40 percent DEET. Bug repellents using other chemicals have come onto the market more recently. Some use derivatives of eucalyptus, which has a more pleasant scent, or various other ingredients.

Once you are finished scouring the woods for morels, you have to be able to navigate back to your vehicle. I found out a long time ago that, despite my fairly good sense of direction, it is quite easy to get turned around when one zigzags through the woods with the eyes probing the ground, not paying particular attention to direction or the position of the sun. In my lifetime I have encountered a host of mushroom hunters who were heading in the wrong direction or were at a loss as to which way to turn. In the early years I just carried a compass, having first set it on a heading pointing back to where I had left my car. You might be surprised at how helpful even an inexpensive compass can be despite the fact that you rarely walk in a straight line. Most of the time I managed to surface from the woods within fifty yards of my car, and even on long, convoluted paths I was at least able to return to the road, leaving me with only the relatively simple decision of whether to go right or left along the road to find the vehicle.

A compass is not hard to use. I prefer an orienteering compass, which has a rotating housing attached to a usually plastic baseplate. The top of the housing generally has the

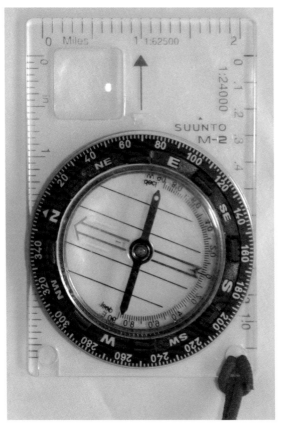

A typical orienteering compass

cardinal points printed on the upper surface and a degree dial around the lower rim. The bottom baseplate has an arrow on one side.

As soon as I leave the car and take a few steps into the woods, I point the arrow—the pointer—in the direction of my parked car and, holding the compass on a level horizontal plane, turn the degree dial until the compass needle covers the orienting arrow on the inside of the compass housing. Once set, I do not move the dial for the duration of the foray. When ready to return to the car, I grasp the compass, holding it level, and turn the compass until the needle, which is often painted red, is again aligned with the arrow on the inside of the compass housing. The arrow painted on the baseplate should point in the direction of the desired return path. Of course, this assumes that I have been moving in a straight line on a constant heading, which is rarely the case. When hunting mushrooms, I tend to zigzag, but fortunately the errors usually cancel each other out; however, if I change my general direction while in the woods, I will need to check the number of degrees I have deviated from the original course and compensate for this when heading back. Surprisingly, I usually still manage to come out close to my destination.

When using a compass, one must make sure the instrument is not in the presence of large metal objects that might deflect the needle away from magnetic north.

I recall the time when a friend of mine almost lost his life due to such a blunder. Heading from Grand Portage, Minnesota, to Isle Royale in a boat with his friends, he started at night when the winds on Lake Superior are usually calm. His ship's compass was not lit; hence, from time to time he used a steel flashlight to illuminate the compass, not realizing that the proximity of the metal mass was causing a significant deflection of the compass needle. It wasn't until daylight that he realized he was heading off course with a significant error.

By then both gas tanks were almost empty. Luckily, one member of the expedition saw what looked like land in the morning fog 90 degrees to their heading and, steering in that direction, they managed to reach their destination.

A more powerful alternative to a compass is a GPS. These days the task of navigation is considerably easier because a GPS is no longer prohibitively expensive and is very easy to carry around one's neck, on a belt, or in a pocket. All one needs to do is mark a waypoint before heading into the woods. Some of the original GPS models had problems acquiring a satellite signal in deep woods or hilly country. The more recent models have pretty much overcome this handicap; furthermore, if a signal is unobtainable, one can always climb to the top of a hill where the acquisition process becomes more reliable. Today's instruments will bring you back to within plus or minus 10 feet of your destination. In fact, the present-day instruments are so accurate that you can use them to mark a particular hunting spot, such as a tree that provided an exceptionally rich harvest, as a waypoint. I still use a compass, though, and carry the GPS primarily as a backup or simply to pinpoint the exact return route, which I can follow using my compass. It saves time.

For some, especially older folks, who tend to hunt primarily along main roads, the issue of navigation is not important. Many "shroomers," including me, prefer to penetrate deeper into the woods where the chances of being preceded by their rivals are lower. Quite often I wind up exploring areas that may be more than a mile or two away from the main road. Going that far isn't always necessary to fill your basket. In fact, in their haste to be the first into the deep forest some hunters miss mushrooms that are right under their noses.

I remember a time a few years ago when I drove my 4×4 vehicle to a spot on a logging road that was just below an elevated plateau with a very high density of ash trees—a productive area that produced good crops of yellow morels year after year. The area was only a few acres in size, so I always tried to arrive early for fear that someone else could easily pick out the area. Having arrived at the spot where I usually pulled off, I saw that another truck had arrived ahead of me. Several young men got out and immediately took off for the ridge, almost running, without exploring the area in between. At first I was sore at myself for not getting up earlier, but I finally decided to head in a different direction. Passing their truck, I spotted a trio of nice yellows no more than 2 feet from the left front tire. Sometimes in our haste we miss the obvious. Quite a few times I have found it unnecessary to go deep into the woods since I could fill my basket not far from my car. I guess many mushroom hunters assume these places will be the first to be picked and don't even bother to look.

But for those who venture deep into the woods the navigational aids are a necessity. Heading for the trees in a zigzag fashion, concentrating on the ground, following logging roads that twist and turn and split into multiple forks can leave one in a predicament when it comes time to head back to the vehicle. Often when hunters realize they are lost, they panic and rush even deeper into the unknown, and this is usually at a time when they are exhausted from walking all day in rough terrain. So carrying a compass is a good idea, and investing in a GPS is even better.

I often go on a foray in the company of my wife and sometimes with the kids. On these occasions, it is a good policy to carry a loud whistle around your neck. Pursuing our own instincts, we often head in different directions and get separated. Having a whistle helps us keep track of one another. Unfortunately, sound doesn't carry as far as you'd think in the woods, so you have to keep in touch before the separation reaches more than 50 yards.

Checklist of Shroomers' Implements

- ❐ Walking stick (light and sturdy)
- ❐ Mosquito repellent (preferably at least 40 percent DEET)
- ❐ Compass or GPS
- ❐ Knife
- ❐ Canvas bag, basket, or other suitable container for mushrooms
- ❐ Raincoat
- ❐ Light, waterproof boots with ridged soles
- ❐ Whistle
- ❐ Walkie-talkie (if hunting with a partner or partners)
- ❐ Map indicating boundaries of public land
- ❐ Drinking water
- ❐ Notebook and pencil
- ❐ Premoistened towelettes

Once again modern electronic technology comes to the rescue. These days we each carry a walkie-talkie, which enables us to communicate once we lose sight of each other. Even an inexpensive walkie-talkie reaches 5 miles these days, and better models reach even farther. Unfortunately, we cannot tell each other where we are should we become separated by a significant distance unless we each also carry a GPS, but at least we can find out if all is well, how we are doing, and when we intend to head back.

All this equipment would be of little help if you had no place to put the mushrooms once you found them. It is essential to carry a bag or some type of basket or container for this purpose. Early in the game, we used to carry a basket. A mushroom basket makes a great depository, but it is a nuisance to carry. Some morel hunters use a potato bag made of netting. This type of bag has the advantage of leaving the mushrooms exposed to the cool air, which reduces spoilage. Dedicated and environmentally conscious morel hunters also claim that the netting allows for scattering of mushroom spores, thus aiding propagation of the species. But the main purpose of this type of container is to keep the mushrooms cool and fresh. I prefer to carry a canvas bag fastened to my belt. I have used paper lunch bags, but these break when they become wet from damp mushrooms or rain, possibly returning the mushrooms to the forest floor. You should never use a plastic bag. Plastic accelerates spoilage, particularly on warm days, so use plastic only to carry a spare pair of socks or this book. Do not use it to carry mushrooms.

A mushroom hunter also needs a knife. We must understand that the mushroom we pick is only the fruiting body of the fungus, the rest of which is underground. The portion that is underground is called the mycelium by mycologists. The mushroom is like a pear, and the mycelium is like the pear tree. The mycelium of the *Morchella* fungus resembles a network of white threads that can be damaged by yanking the mushroom up by the "roots." It is for this reason that a responsible mushroom hunter gently cuts off the mushroom without disturbing the mycelium, which may provide another crop of fruiting bodies later that week or next season. Doing this makes one a good guardian of the bounty that nature provides. Damaging the mycelium is akin to breaking the branches of the pear tree while harvesting the fruit. A broken branch will not yield fruit, and a damaged mycelium will take time to repair itself. This network of mycelium often covers whole acres of ground while the fruiting body, the mushroom, only surfaces in certain favorable places when the conditions for reproduction—that is, for releasing the spores that the wind carries to new places—are just right. The best practice is to cut off the mushroom about half an inch above the ground to minimize the damage to the mycelium. It is also helpful in keeping your morels clean since the part of the stem that was in the ground carries sand, soil, and other debris that can contaminate the rest of your find. It is a good idea to tie the pocket knife to your basket or collection bag since laying it on the ground is often a prescription for losing it among the trees.

For those who want to try mushroom photography, I recommend carrying a light space blanket and a tripod in addition to your camera and the usual accessories. The aluminized space blanket comes in handy, particularly when the ground is wet and one needs to lie down in order to get a good shot from a "mole's-eye view." It is also handy to sit on come lunchtime. Although modern digital cameras take very good pictures even under poor light conditions, a tripod is necessary to get a decent depth of field. The photographer

At the end of a day, a basket of black morels

has to shoot using a small aperture, hence a longer exposure. Without the tripod, the picture will frequently be out of focus.

Finally, I like to carry a few moist towelettes in my pocket. Handling morels soils your hands, and they need to be wiped clean now and then.

These are the basic items one needs to carry on a mushroom hunt. For those wives or husbands who simply wait in the car—a spouse who does not yet share your mushrooming passion—a good book is one more item to complete the checklist.

When Do We Go
Morel Hunting?

Morels are early spring mushrooms. In the northern tiers of the country, under normal weather conditions and with sufficient moisture and warmth, morels start coming out about the second week of May. In other parts of the country the date of season opening is subject to fairly significant disparity, and there is always some fluctuation from year to year. I have endeavored to provide an approximate timetable on the map at the end of this chapter with the following reserva-

A sure sign it's time to go . . .

tion: while morels in any particular part of the country exhibit fair consistency with respect to the time of the year they make their appearance, we must recognize that the timing of the growth season is not only dependent on geography, that is, the latitude of the region in question, but on a host of other variables. This initial period of growth is influenced by such factors as the microclimate, which, in turn, is a function of the area's relative topography and precipitation (amount, frequency, and timing with respect to the mushroom's growth cycle). The cycle is also affected by whether the area has a continental or maritime climate.

When I arrive at the hunting grounds, I usually look for visible signs that the right time has arrived. In the Midwest, these signs include the blooming of spring flowers such as trilliums, Dutchman's-breeches, and Virginia bluebells. I may not be able to forecast the date, but I can usually sense that spring has arrived and it is time to go and look.

The first mushroom species to emerge is usually the *Verpa conica*, followed by black morels and *Verpa bohemica*. Again, under normal conditions the life span of a flush of black morels is about ten days, less if there are heavy rains or it is very warm. High temperatures accelerate the fruition process, shortening the life span of a mushroom. Occasional stragglers pop up later. Following the black morels, and often overlapping, are the grays. Within a week of the grays, I usually see yellow morels—the delectable *Morchella esculenta*— and they have a life span of about two weeks. However, as mentioned earlier, sometimes I see a late flush of the giant yellow morels, which in Michigan and Wisconsin may arrive after Memorial Day and can persist well into June.

The farther south one goes, the earlier the season. In Illinois, Kentucky, and Missouri the proper time to start looking is toward the end of April, and for roughly every three hundred miles farther south one starts looking a week

Morel Hunters' Timetable

Zone **1** March 15–April 15
Zone **2** April 10–May 10
Zone **3** May 10–May 31
Zone **4** May 15 and later, depending on elevation

or two earlier. All of this presupposes normal weather conditions. The worst enemy of a good crop is the lack of snow in winter up north or lack of rain early in the spring. Under conditions of extreme drought, there may be no flush at all. During moderately dry weather the crop may be limited to a few stragglers growing in scattered locations that had better access to moisture.

The second prerequisite for a decent crop is temperature. It must not be too frigid nor too warm. When the weather turns too warm too early, dense vegetation springs up. The sun cannot penetrate and warm the soil, and, therefore, the mushroom crop is meager. Also, the mushrooms are hard to see beneath all the vegetation. Mushrooms, like all living things, have an internal clock; if conditions are not favorable when it's their time to fruit, there will be no flush, even if conditions improve later. If they miss the window of opportunity—the period when their internal clock is programmed for growth—the mushroom will wait until the alarm clock rings again next year.

While the flush will not start if the nights are too cold and frosty, it has been my experience that once the fungus starts the fruiting process an occasional cold snap or even a frost will not jeopardize the flush. The growth may slow down or pause temporarily, but it will continue when conditions improve.

On the other hand, once the mushroom has started to grow, the mycelium underneath needs continuous access to moisture. If the growth is interrupted by a dry spell, the mushroom will shrivel up and dry before it sees the light of day.

This entire schedule depends on a number of variables and, as with other rules in life, has its exceptions. While the morel is a spring mushroom, a couple of years ago I found a solitary black morel in northern Colorado in July, and just last year I discovered several black morels in the mountains of the Snowy Range of southeastern Wyoming in the middle of August. All were healthy even though they woke up late. In the mountains, snow often does not melt until the middle of June, so a later flush is not completely unexpected; however, I would never have believed August morels had I not seen them with my own eyes. I guess even nature's internal clock breaks down sometimes.

Like anything else in nature, there are favorable and unfavorable conditions for growth. One of the favorable conditions that may somewhat alter the regular growth schedule is fire. It has often been stated that if a forest experiences fire there will be an abundant crop of morels the following season. This assertion was proven several years ago when, due to extreme drought and high temperatures, there were a number of devastating forest fires in the western states—particularly in Idaho, Washington, Oregon, and California. The following year there were phenomenal crops of morels in many of the burned out locations. There were even rumors to the

This morel had to do some heavy weight lifting . . .

You've got a set of twins . . .

A rather rare occurrence: a yellow morel in the open

effect that some fires were started by commercial morel pickers. I certainly hope that such stories are not true. The occurrence of enormous fruitings of morels the spring following a
fire seems to be particularly prevalent in the western states.
No one is quite sure why a forest fire should promote a

healthy flush of mushrooms. One theory asserts that the fungus benefits from the minerals locked in the ashes of trees. Others are of the opinion that a burned out forest allows for more sunlight, which warms the soil.

You should also be aware that morels often pop up in huge quantities around certain types of dying trees.

Some years ago the northern tiers of the country contained a vast number of elms. These trees, *Ulmus americana*, were attacked by a fungus, *Ceratocystis ulmi*. The fungus causes Dutch elm disease, which killed a large number of the trees. The disease was introduced on the East Coast in the 1930s. It gradually spread, and by the 1970s it had wiped out most of the elms in the eastern third of the country. The areas around these dying trees became treasured sites for morel hunters. I recall one spring day some ten years ago when I stumbled on an area around a quarter acre in size on which there were half a dozen fairly young dying elms. I started to search, found about seventy yellow morels, and promptly marked the spot as a waypoint on my GPS. I visited the same site the following year and gathered over thirty mushrooms. The year after the number was reduced to less than ten, and in subsequent years there was no sign that morels had ever grown in that spot. I have heard theories that since mushrooms live in a symbiotic relationship with the roots of certain trees, they thrive when the tree starts to die because the roots no longer have to supply nutrients to the tree; however, eventually the root system dies, and the mycelium dies along with it. This seems to make sense. By now the vast majority of the elms have perished, and morel hunters have had to turn their sights elsewhere.

Despite all the variables, morels usually start to grow in a given location within about a week (plus or minus) of the average date. For the shroomer who undertakes a lengthy trip, it is advisable to count on this seasonal variance and figure on having to spend a few extra days if the start of the season is early

A solitary *esculenta*

or delayed. I like to arrive a few days before the average season opening day, which does not occur in all the locations at exactly the same time. This gives me time to reconnoiter my favored areas for signs of logging or other disturbances so that when the mushrooms do begin to emerge, I can be there before the best locations are picked. There is nothing more disappointing to a mushroom hunter than seeing freshly cut stems, indicating that an early riser has already been there.

To establish the beginning of the growth season with greater probability, I check the weather conditions in the desired hunting area on the Internet or call some local friends who can brief me on the weather. But nothing beats being close to your staked out hunting area and being able to saunter into the woods for inspection.

Due to these weather variables, the probability of success diminishes proportionally to the fewer days available for the trip. I usually plan on a minimum of ten days, preferably two weeks or more, to make sure that I will be on location throughout the main growing season. For working people this may be problematic, but I don't like to hear the locals say, "Oh, you should have been here last week. People were picking them by the bushel." Nor do I want to have to leave before the season begins. Timing is essential to success. Unfortunately, it is difficult to second-guess nature.

So, Where Do We Start Looking?

This is the real reason you bought this book, right? So, let us get started! First of all, as every hunter knows, your quarry must reside in the general area in which you intend to hunt. This is also true of mushrooms. Every mushroom depends on some substance for its sustenance. Most mushrooms are saprophytes—that is, they live on decaying matter. *Coprinus comatus* (shaggy cap, inky cap), for instance, lives off decaying leaf litter and animal excrement. *Agaricus bisporus* (the white mushrooms that are cultivated and available in grocery

A group of black morels in leaf litter

stores) thrives on horse manure. I used to go to a field in the fall that was used as polo grounds on weekends. Lots of horses translated into lots of mushrooms. Other mushrooms live in a symbiotic relationship with certain trees. *Boletus edulis* (king bolete, porcini, cep) is found around firs, spruces, and pines while morels usually grow in deciduous forests among maple, ash, elm, and beech trees, and in apple orchards. Each species has its own preference; hence, we must use this knowledge as a starting point when we go looking for morels.

Before we decide in what general area we should start looking, we must ensure that our target hunting grounds have mature trees of the right kind and that these trees are located on public land such as state parks and state forests. National parks do not allow the picking of any growing things—flowers or mushrooms—and some national forests are beginning to require permits. On private land one needs to secure the owner's permission. Because different species of morels keep company with specific species of trees, our search for suitable hunting grounds must start by driving around to locate areas with these trees. In northern Michigan, morel hunting is concentrated primarily around the communities of Mesic, near Cadillac, and then farther north around Kalkaska, Grayling, Gaylord, Traverse City, Boyne City, Boyne Falls, and even across the Mackinac Bridge in the Upper Peninsula. These areas not only contain the right species of trees but they also have large tracts of accessible public land. In Wisconsin, morels are found around Devil's Lake State Park, along the Mississippi, and in other areas. In Illinois and Iowa, some of the prime areas are also along the shores of the Mississippi River. Other prominent sites in the Midwest are in central Illinois. I've read that morels are found in every state of the union. While I think one would have a hard time locating a crop in some of the arid sections of the Southwest, I do believe that morels are more wide-spread than we suspect. (See the Web site mushroomexpert .com for morel ranges and maps.)

Since each individual species of morel lives near certain types of trees, we must concentrate our search on the areas where these particular trees appear. Sometimes such preferences are particular to a certain region, but this is still a good starting point.

Let's begin with the black morel since it is one of the first to appear and it is less choosy when it comes to tree preference. As mentioned earlier, the habitat of black morels is not confined to one species of tree, as it is with the gray and yellow varieties. In my experience one has the best chance of finding blacks in the previous year's leaf litter under maple and beech trees. The soil should be well drained and rich in humus and the leaf litter fairly deep.

Since morels begin to pop up before many trees have leafed out, we must be able to recognize trees by their bark. Beeches are quite easy to spot. Their light gray, smooth bark stands out in the spring forest. Maples are a bit more difficult to identify by the bark since it is quite similar to that of other trees such as the American basswood. When the tree is young, the bark of a sugar maple may also be fairly smooth, but mature maples are darker gray and roughly furrowed with medium-sized ridges. The Norway maple has similar bark, often darker gray to brown with more pronounced ridges. However, maples are easy to recognize since they open their leaf buds early. One can identify them by their five-lobed, pointed, dark green leaves, which, in the case of the silver maple, are silvery white on the underside.

While this is the predominant habitat of the black morel, the mushroom is not bound to these trees alone. Another species around which many black morels might be located is the poplar (or "popple" as it is sometimes called in Michigan).

The trunk of a beech

An adult sugar maple

The bark of the white (or silver) poplar is very light gray and smooth, but it becomes rougher, especially at the base, as the tree reaches adulthood. I once collected 175 black morels among ferns and fairly young poplars with no other trees in sight. Another species of tree that may be mixed with the maples and beeches is the American basswood. The bark of the basswood is rather difficult to distinguish from that of the maple, but this is of little importance since the black morel thrives equally among both species. There are still other species, such as apples and elms, that testify to the fact that the black morel is not as finicky as its gray and yellow siblings.

The fact that the black morel is most often found under the trees that have been mentioned does not say that one will not find it in another environment. There was a spot not far from the Mackinac Bridge, which connects the Lower and Upper Peninsulas of Michigan, where my wife and I would find nice, large, black morels on one side of a logging road. This area consisted of mature poplars mixed with maples. One bright morning we visited the area and within a couple of hours collected a sufficient quantity of mushrooms before lunch. Prior to lunch I decided to take a quick look at an area across the road that was densely populated with young spruce trees. Upon entering, I almost fell over with disbelief. The ground under the low branches of the spruces was literally covered with morels. There were hundreds. I could have filled a bathtub in less than a half hour. We had been hunting just thirty yards from the spot across the logging road for years, and it had never occurred to us to look under the evergreens. Unfortunately, we already had our limit, and, furthermore, we could never have carried such a haul. The next year we headed immediately into the conifer area, but there were no morels, though we did find them across the road among the poplars. There are many such stories testifying to the fact that the black morel is a wily, unpredictable creature. Unlike

The bark of an American basswood

the gray and the yellow varieties, black morels do not necessarily appear in the same location in subsequent years. A place
with an abundant crop one year might be a barren forest floor
the next, and a new patch might materialize just thirty yards
from there. In general, the ideal place to look is under the
beech, maple, and poplar trees where there is a bare or
sparsely vegetated forest floor and ample leaf litter from the
previous fall. Black morels tend to avoid dense ground vege-

tation such as patches of wild leeks, trilliums, and other spring flowers. Perhaps this is because such vegetation prevents the sun from warming the soil. This is a good thing, however, since the blacks tend to stand out and are easier to spot in leaf litter.

Evidently, black morels don't want to play by a rigid set of rules. Yet there are some general characteristics of their preferred habitat, as we have noted.

There is another frequent controversy among morel hunters concerning the topography of the terrain: should one look for the mushrooms along the tops of ridges or in the valleys below? I have not been able to get a definitive answer to this question from my hunting friends, but my own tendency is to concentrate on the ridges early in the season and in the valleys later on. However, I do not rely solely on this rule. In fact, each time I advance a theory about black morels, I run into exceptions almost immediately. Thus, I was not surprised when several times I found a patch of blacks among ferns with the nearest tree the length of a football field away. They do like to play games with you.

When one sees a black morel close-up, it may seem as if they would be easy to spot from a distance. This is not always so. They are often so well camouflaged that they are easily overlooked. There are many dead branches poking out of the leaves, and they resemble the tips of black morels enough that one is lured away from the real quarry to waste time checking out sticks. Yet the successful hunter must explore each likely location slowly and thoroughly unless he or she wants to leave some mushrooms behind for future reproduction. Early in the season, some young black morels may still be buried beneath the leaves, so one needs to check all suspicious bumps and piles. Yet there are always a few mushrooms left behind. Even the experienced and careful morel hunter will miss a few. I have been with friends who propose to move into another location if there is any evidence that a competitor has visited our "spot" before us. I tend to explore the area anyway. Most of the time I still find enough mushrooms to make the exercise worthwhile. And I am sure I also leave a few for those who come after me. Morels are fun to hunt. It is often rigorous, but we are compensated with aromatic supplements for our kitchen, fresh air, plenty of exercise, and the satisfaction of successfully responding to the challenge nature has presented—the game of hide and seek.

Hunting gray and yellow morels makes tree identification more essential since these mushrooms, for the most part, live in a symbiotic relationship with a particular species of tree— the ash (white ash in particular). In fact 98 percent of the grays and yellows I find in Michigan are located within an eight-foot radius of a mature ash, often literally within inches of the trunk. When I hunt the *Morchella deliciosa* and *esculenta*, I proceed from one ash to the next completely ignoring other species. Occasionally, I find a loner near a maple or other tree species, but this is clearly an exception to the rule since the groups and clusters are almost invariably in the immediate vicinity of ashes, at least in the northern Great Lakes states.

This, of course, makes it mandatory to be able to spot an ash tree from some distance even though this particular tree buds out late. In the middle of May the buds are just beginning to open, so hunters are unable to use the leaves for identification. Furthermore, ash trees do not usually have low-hanging branches, so any leaves that may be out early are high in the tree's crown.

Fortunately, the bark of an ash tree is quite distinct, as is evident in the photos that follow, and after some practice you will become proficient at spotting the tree from a relatively great distance. The trunk is dark gray, almost black when wet, and it is visibly darker than other trees. It is also deeply furrowed with elongated diamond-shaped ridges.

Typical habitat of black morels

Twin black morels peeking out of leaf litter

An ash in a mixed deciduous forest

Close-up of an ash trunk

A Michigan ash just leafing out in late May

Ash trees usually stand out. This is important, as it will allow you the maximum use of the time available and the maximum probability of a rich harvest. Once the ash is identified, the real "hide and seek" game ensues. When approaching the tree, one must tread carefully since the grays and yellows often grow under more prolific vegetation. In northern Michigan, where the soil is of a sandy humus composition, this vegetation consists of the leaves of wild leeks, trilliums, Dutchman's-breeches, various species of fern, and other plants. In other parts of the Midwest there is a noticeable presence of Virginia bluebells and other spring flowers. If we arrive at a location before a competitor, we may see a mature morel growing in the open. Many times, however, we need to find mushrooms that are just coming up or well hidden, possibly missed by a hunter who has already scoured the area. Here is where a good stick comes in handy. The gray and yellow morels are particularly adept at hiding. I've frequently found upward of thirty young morels within an 8-foot radius of a tree even though not a single mushroom was initially visible. It is always a good idea to approach the tree carefully to avoid stepping on well-hidden mushrooms. Use a stick to lift up the vegetation in a systematic manner until you are fairly sure you have located every concealed mushroom around the tree. This is time consuming, but it becomes even more important once you find one or two mushrooms. The presence of one morel hints at the possibility of a group of them. They may be all on one side of the tree or scattered around it. Once again, at the beginning of the growth season, some mushrooms may still be under the leaves. The ones whose growth has advanced a bit may begin to lift up a leaf pile forming a more or less visible bump. Sometimes the bump is simply hiding a part of a fallen tree limb, but often the bump yields a family of young mushrooms.

It is also important to be observant and note if there is a pattern to the direction in which the mushrooms are found with respect to the tree trunk. It is my theory that in the early, cool part of the season one can best find morels in places where the sun has been able to penetrate, defrost, and warm the soil. During the last few years, I've noticed that in several locations, which happened to be on a steep slope facing southwest, I've found a majority of the mushrooms on the southwest side of the tree trunk. It wasn't a totally dependable observation, but it was true in a statistically significant number of cases.

The only plausible explanation is that only the southwest side of the tree had access to afternoon sun while the morning sun was shielded by the interfering hill. These areas would receive generous warmth, whereas the east and northeast sides would be in almost constant shade. When I found mushrooms around a particular tree, I found them southwest of the tree trunk seven out of ten times. I did not neglect the other directions, since I occasionally found them there as well, but the observation allowed me to concentrate my search on a smaller area, which allowed me to examine a larger number of trees. So even keeping track of the microgeography of a find can increase the probability of discovering the hiding places of the wily morel.

One more clue: substantial flushes of morels often appear in an area that has been "disturbed" in some manner. From time to time, I find groups of mushrooms in the middle of a recently created logging road or where a bulldozer has ventured in and scraped the soil. This is an interesting phenomenon since, given what we know about mycelium, one might think that such disturbances would destroy the fungal network, requiring years of healing and rebuilding.

Also interesting is the fact that such disturbances do not create long-term mushroom havens. The bonanza tends to evaporate after a season or two. I have met mushroom hunters who, taking advantage of this phenomenon, confine their forays mainly to logging roads, never venturing more than a few feet away.

It is a good idea to keep track of the general location of a find. Nobody is able to pinpoint one tree in a forest covering a number of square miles, but with a GPS one can certainly find his or her way back to within 20 or 30 feet of the tree. I say this because, under favorable conditions, new mushrooms can pop up almost overnight. I recently hunted an area less than a quarter of a square mile in size five days in a row and found enough mushrooms each day to make it unnecessary to change venues. I know for a fact that many of these mushrooms were growing around the same trees where I had found morels earlier. This was despite the fact that a morel requires several days to develop from the "fetal" stage to a full-grown specimen. The only explanation for this is that these mushrooms were already at an advanced stage of development when I first visited their birthplace but were hidden from view, remaining undiscovered despite a thorough search, and only later poked out of their hiding places.

Thus, it is of some value to keep track of the location of notable finds on a daily basis and to keep coming back. A GPS, notebook, and pencil is all you need to satisfy this requirement. A good memory is of even more help. This is not just because a new, young flush may come up overnight; it is also because every mushroom hunter leaves a few behind. Very often I retrace my steps, stop at the same trees that yielded a better than average harvest, and invariably, find a few stragglers that I missed.

Another characteristic of the yellow morels is that they tend to come up around the same ash trees over and over for a number of years, unlike black morels, which may come up in a given location in huge quantities one season and not appear again for a decade.

A few years ago my wife and I ran into a bonanza of black morels in an area where we usually find the yellow variety. It was an area no larger than 20 by 30 feet, yet we collected enough mushrooms by ten o'clock in the morning to call it a day. The trophy was so abundant that I have been going back to this particular area each year since. To my great disappointment, I have not found a single black morel there since that time. I did find a few gray ones the year before last. So returning to the same spots when hunting gray or yellow morels often pays dividends, but this is not necessarily the

Some morels grow large

case with the blacks. They make us search for them over and over again. Nevertheless, while they do not fruit in exactly the same location, they are certainly more consistent within the same general area.

It's quite another story with the grays and yellows unless somebody cuts down a particular tree. In one favored location of mine there was a huge old ash tree, perhaps 5 feet in diameter, right next to an unused logging road. For six years in a row, I have collected between thirty and fifty-five yellow morels within a radius of about 8 feet of the huge trunk. I could count on it and often headed for that tree first, which was easy to find since it was at the top of a hill just inches from the old road. Three years ago loggers cut it down, much to my chagrin. The following season I still found about twenty mushrooms. Last year there were only three. I doubt that I will find any this coming May.

While grays and yellows are found predominantly near ash trees—at least east of the Rockies—there is another species that morel hunters have fervently sought for years, the elm. As noted earlier, the American elm was attacked by Dutch elm disease (probably so-called because it was thought to have been imported to the United States accidently from the Netherlands). It is now believed that it was introduced to Europe from Asia during World War I. It gradually spread across the European continent, killing thousands of elms. Ultimately, it affected Great Britain and then the United States. As the malady spread, people noticed that hundreds of yellow morels were frequently popping up in the area covered by the root system of the dying tree. Interestingly, the yellow morel thrives around live ash trees and stops growing when the ash dies or is cut down. Just the opposite is true in the case of the elm. Go figure! You will not find a yellow morel next to an unaffected elm tree, but a dying one is suddenly surrounded by a sumptuous crop of mushrooms. It is another piece of evidence testifying to the inscrutable nature of this mushroom. It not only challenges us physically but forces us to play a chess game, constantly augmenting our knowledge of its behavior through experience. Then we must logically arrange the individual observations into some "rules of thumb."

Unfortunately, most of the American elms died. Those that survive are of little help to the morel hunter. It was not many years ago that my wife and I ran into an area about 30 by 50 feet in size that was literally sprouting with yellow morels. When the excitement of the discovery passed, I started to examine the trees and discovered that they were fairly young elms that were dying. Most still had their leaves, but they looked sickly and the trees were obviously in trouble. We collected about seventy-five mushrooms scattered over the area. I marked the spot and decided to keep coming back to get more. The next spring, the trees appeared to be dead. We still found about twenty-five morels. The following year I found a solitary straggler, and after that not a single mushroom was to be seen.

Regrettably, the same misfortune may befall the ash tree. Recently, parts of the Midwest have been infested with an insect known as the emerald ash borer. It is a sucking insect. Its jaws penetrate the plant tissue of an ash and feed on the cell liquid. The leaves eventually curl up, and the tree dies. Fortunately, there appears to be help on the horizon. The tree can be treated before the infestation occurs. "Starting early is the key," says David Smitley, a Michigan State University entomologist. The treatment must begin as soon as the insect appears in an area and before it attacks any tree. This can work on a small plot of private property, but will the state invest in treating thousands of trees? Or will they just cut them down for lumber?

In northern Michigan, as elsewhere, many of the mature ash trees have been cut down by loggers. This reduces the attractiveness of the area for a morel hunter since yellow morels prefer mature ash and are less often found around trees less than 10 inches in diameter. Should this reduction in ash density be augmented by the devastation caused by the ash borer, it would be a blow to the morel hunter. If there are no ash trees, the number of hunters will be reduced, which would have a harmful effect on the area's businesses.

As was mentioned earlier, another good place to find morels is in apple orchards, particularly orchards with old, perhaps exhausted and dying, trees. This is, of course, more difficult for the out-of-state mushroomer since orchards are usually on private property. Now and then I run into old orchards, usually around abandoned settlements. A few years ago I discovered one such place west of Traverse City, Michigan. Not much was left of the old homestead, but there were a few old apple trees, by now mostly overgrown with young maples. A few offered nothing, but one or two of the trees were surrounded by nice yellow morels. Once again, what surprised me was the fact that the homestead was obviously abandoned, the apple trees were so old they no longer produced fruit, and yet there were occasional, albeit limited, flushes of mushrooms under some of the trees.

We also find morels in other odd places. Many years ago, when I first started to hunt morels seriously, I found a nice group in an unexpected place. Besides hunting and photographing mushrooms, I do wildflower photography. This particular day I was shooting yellow lady's slippers (*Cypripedium calceolus*) in the vicinity of Devil's Lake State Park in Wisconsin. Walking back along railroad tracks to shorten the distance to my car, I almost stepped on a huge morel growing next to a railroad tie. A quick inspection revealed about a dozen more mushrooms all within roughly 3 feet of the railroad bed. Thinking that I had just made a significant discovery that would dramatically increase my find average, I started to systematically explore much of Wisconsin's railroad net until I began to limp even when walking on a straight, paved road. Needless to say, the number of mushrooms I found per mile of exploration was far lower than what I would have gathered had I been walking at random into any bushy or wooded area in that state or the other forty-nine.

This again underlines the assertion that morel locations, like the outcome of a football match, cannot be predicted with certainty. We can examine all the statistics, and they are of great help as one source of guidance, but we are unable to draw definitive instructions from them regarding the location and timing of our next find. And perhaps it's just as well. Being able to predict exact locations and times would rob us of the excitement of suspense and discovery.

And everything I have written here is of value, and it will materially increase your chances for a successful morel hunt. This is despite the fact that in other parts of the United States—west of the Rocky Mountains, for example—morels behave in a somewhat different manner. Life is not long enough for one man to acquire the same depth of experience in widely dispersed locations. It takes years of experience to become familiar with all the hunting grounds in just one county let alone in all fifty states.

Despite all the threats to the survival of morels, there are still plenty of places where they thrive and will continue to do so for the foreseeable future. With knowledge and patience, we can still enjoy the healthy and exciting craft of the mushroom hunt.

How Do We Preserve the Find?

Now that we know where and how to find mushrooms, we need to learn about preserving what we bring back. There are a number of ways, some better than others. Some of my fellow morel hunters simply place their booty in an ice cooler and cook and eat them when they get home. The mushrooms will survive several days, perhaps even longer, in a cooler or refrigerator. But what if you can't eat all you found and you want to have a ready supply until next season or even longer?

Another set of triplets

Some hunters simply take them as they are and freeze them whole. I have never tried freezing them in this manner, but I don't like this method for several reasons. First, most people do not have enough room in their freezers. Whole mushrooms take up an enormous amount of space, and it is wasted space since morels are hollow and they would be freezing a lot of empty air. Furthermore, morels, a product of the woods, often provide housing for undesirable creatures such as slugs and bugs of various kinds. I am not a vegetarian, but I am turned off by the thought of consuming such critters along with the delectable mushrooms. So this is what my wife and I do. Immediately upon returning from the hunt, I set out to clean the mushrooms. I first gently remove any foreign material with a soft mushroom brush, and I then blow off loose particles of grass or other organic matter. I next slice each mushroom in half longitudinally and inspect the inside for unwanted residents, removing them forcefully if they don't vacate the premises voluntarily. Then it's my wife's turn. She places a handful at a time into a buttered frying pan—in a single layer only since more will cause the mushrooms to be steamed instead of sautéed—and sautés them just as they are—no salt, no spices, and just enough butter to saturate the mushrooms. Salt and spices are not added since salt tends to degrade the tissue of the mushrooms when they are in long-term storage. The mushrooms are turned once and kept over the hot stove until all the liquid is gone. We occasionally add an additional tablespoon of butter before turning them. After the mushrooms cool, we place appropriate quantities in plastic freezer bags, just enough for a meal in each bag, and store them in the freezer. By cutting the mushrooms in half and sautéing them, the volume is reduced by about five to one. When the mushrooms are defrosted, even after several years, they are just as if they were freshly picked and processed. The sautéing not only reduces the volume but it destroys the enzymes that tend to decompose the body of the mushroom when it is kept longer than a few days.

We do not recommend washing morels in water to clean them. They are truly sponges and immediately absorb water, and once they absorb water their quality is degraded.

Freezer space is limited in our trailer, and for that reason we initially tried to dehydrate the mushrooms. We commonly use this practice with firm mushrooms such as king boletes (*Boletus edulis*). The results are quite satisfactory for boletes. With morels, however, the mushrooms are not as good upon rehydration as with the sautéing and freezing method. Of course, the advantage is that they can be stored in a tightly sealed jar and don't take up space in the freezer. A number of electric dehydrators are available in small appli-

Ready for the kitchen. Note that the mushrooms have been cut in half and cleaned.

ance stores, but we still prefer the sautéing and freezing method for long-term preservation.

Many areas in which morels grow are sandy. It is not unusual, therefore, to bring home mushrooms that have retained some sand in the pits. This sand is quite difficult to remove, and eating mushrooms with embedded sand grains is very unpleasant.

I recall one year when we decided to go to a restaurant to sample a meal made of freshly picked morels. Even though the meal was well prepared, we could not finish it because of the sand. The gritty sand stayed in our mouths until we rinsed them out with several glasses of water. If the sand cannot be brushed out or blown off, it might be necessary to wash the mushrooms under a stream of running water. I would only wash them if I were unsuccessful at removing the grains of sand by other methods. There is nothing more lamentable than biting into a savory bit of a mushroom and hearing that distinct crunching noise of the gritty grains of sand. Growing up as a child in the Czech Republic, I often watched women feeding geese and ducks and giving them some sand, allegedly to clean their digestive tracts. But that practice is for the birds, and I would just as well have my mushrooms without the grit. My digestion is just fine, thank-you!

Some people pickle their mushrooms. This works great with boletes, the *Grifolas*, and other mushrooms, but I have never acquired a taste for pickled morels. So I recommend that if you want to keep what you cannot eat fresh, use the sautéing and freezing method. It truly preserves morels, and nearly all mushrooms, for a long time in a freshlike condition. The sautéed and frozen mushrooms are very easy to use later, especially if you freeze individual portions that you plan to use in one meal. A few minutes in a pan and it's as if you just collected them in the woods.

The second preferred method is drying. Growing up in

A handsome group of eight *esculentas*

Central Europe, we did not have the modern conveniences that exist today and used to dry our mushrooms by spreading them on a cloth and placing it in the sun. Today there is an array of dehydrators that do the job even when it's not possible to dry the mushrooms outside. The mushrooms are best when dehydrated at about 100°F and not much higher. One must, however, get rid of every last molecule of moisture because the mushrooms will become moldy if they are not absolutely dry. We also prefer to store dry mushrooms in glass containers equipped with a sound rubber gasket on the lid. Plastic bags are only okay for a short time because the closure is often not a hermetical seal.

There is one more thing to remember if you are going to use this method of preservation. It is not sufficient to rehydrate morels prior to use. All members of this genus must be cooked prior to ingestion to prevent gastrointestinal distress. When we sauté the mushrooms, this precaution is taken care of. Dehydrated mushrooms should be cooked prior to placing them on the dinner plate.

There are several other ways to preserve mushrooms, namely, canning and freezing in a container of water such as a cardboard milk container. The former is a lot of work. Furthermore, one needs to beware of botulism when using this method. If you decide to can, be sure to use a pressure cooker. Under pressure the temperature of the water in a cooker reaches well above 212°F in open air, and this high temperature is more likely to destroy any bacteria that could grow into a harmful colony otherwise.

As to freezing in water, there are several reasons to avoid this method. First of all, it occupies a huge amount of space in the freezer. Second, it takes a long time to defrost such a container. And when it does defrost the mushrooms are soggy. They do not sauté well, and if they are fried until all the water evaporates they tend to become rubbery and tough.

Dehydrated mushrooms in jars

So, for my money, I prefer cleaning the mushrooms as soon as they are brought home. By cutting the mushroom off instead of pulling it out of the ground, as I suggested in a prior chapter, there is the added advantage of not contaminating the rest of the mushrooms with dirt, which is hard to remove from the pits. Then you can sauté them in butter, place them in the freezer in sealed plastic bags, and furnish them with a descriptive label indicating the date and place of collection.

We have used mushrooms preserved in this fashion several years after picking them, and we haven't run across a batch that would display a discernible difference from freshly processed mushrooms. Furthermore, from the standpoint of the cook, this is a much faster process once we decide to use them. The frozen contents of a bag of sautéed mushrooms defrost quickly in a frying pan, can be seasoned to taste, and can be used within minutes of removal from the freezer.

About the Edibility
of Mushrooms

There is a considerable amount of apprehension in America about eating mushrooms. The reason for this apprehension is a lack of knowledge. In most of Europe, especially in Eastern and Central Europe and Italy, education about wild mushrooms begins in childhood. Many Europeans gather wild mushrooms as a culinary addition to their dining table, as a dietary supplement to promote health, and as an inexpensive family activity in which the entire family can go trudging through the woods gathering wild fruits such as mushrooms, strawberries, blueberries, and cranberries. As a result of this early education, a European is generally quite knowledgeable about the edible varieties of mushrooms as well as the dangers of the poisonous varieties.

I grew up in the Czech Republic, and as a young boy I spent most weekends during the summer and fall with my parents visiting my uncle and aunt on their farm in a small village not far from my hometown. We either went to one of the lakes for a swim or into the woods to look for what nature offered. Mushrooms were our ultimate quarry, so ever since childhood I have been acquiring the knowledge of generations as to what to look for and what not to touch.

These are not the ways of our modern generations; hence, there is a lack of knowledge, which, in turn, perpetuates the air of witchcraft and danger and the fear of mysterious "toadstools." This is regrettable since such activities in

A trio of yellow morels

nature are a source of education for children. And yet, in view of this lack of knowledge, the apprehension is quite appropriate. Although just a small fraction of the several thousand species of mushrooms in North America are poisonous, it is not wise to play Russian roulette with mushroom poisoning.

Fortunately, the morel family contains species that are readily identifiable, and the danger of getting ill from eating morels is quite low provided that one has at least the basic information about what to pick and what to avoid.

True morels are rarely a source of gastrointestinal problems given two caveats. Morels should not be eaten raw, and one should establish that he or she is not allergic to this genus or mushrooms in general. It is best to eat only a small test quantity initially. There is danger, but it is confined primarily to the category generally referred to as "false morels."

I have already discussed the "cap" mushroom, *Verpa bohemica*. Although this mushroom is often harvested by locals,

A rare globular head of a black morel

especially in Michigan, caution is recommended because in some individuals "an immoderate ingestion can cause some temporary but uncomfortable muscular incoordination."[1]

Even locals who pick this mushroom use only the detachable cap, and the mushroom is well cooked and eaten in reasonable quantities. I avoid picking this species not because the danger of ingesting it is high but because, in my opinion, the mushroom is not as good as its true morel siblings.

---

1. Gary Lincoff, *Simon and Schuster's Guide to Mushrooms* (New York: Simon and Schuster, 1982), 281.

No gastrointestinal problems have been reported for its related species, *Verpa conica*. However, this species is rarely found during the true morel growing season. While there is no apparent danger of toxicity, the mushroom is of substandard culinary value.

The real problem is with the false morel genus *Gyromitra*. While some species of this genus are eaten safely in the United States and many are eaten in Europe, several, such as *Gyromitra esculenta*, *G. brunnea*, and *G. californica*, are usually described as poisonous. Concerning the collection of some of these species in Europe or elsewhere, one must bear in mind that toxicity within the same mushroom species often varies by region. Some species of mushrooms are edible in one part of the world and poisonous elsewhere. Several years ago I ran across a newspaper article reporting that several Vietnamese immigrants had been treated for mushroom poisoning in a hospital after apparently ingesting a North American species of a mushroom they ordinarily picked and ate in their home country. Nor should one rely on the fact that certain mushrooms are eaten by critters such as squirrels. Often animals can tolerate a toxin that is harmful to humans. Late in the summer one often runs across a toxic species of mushroom such as the fly agaric (*Amanita muscaria*) partially eaten by forest critters with no apparent ill effects. Yet we know that such species are toxic and harmful to man.

While cooking some species destroys their toxins, this is not true in general. In some species the toxins survive the cooking process unimpaired; hence, we cannot rely on cooking to render any species harmless. A number of severe poisoning cases have been reported even though the mushrooms in question were well cooked.

Although not all the toxins contained in mushrooms of the *Gyromitra* genus are completely known or understood, medical mycologists have identified one of them as "monomethylhydrazine (MMH) which in the bloodstream causes severe gastrointestinal disturbance and, in some cases, death."[2] This substance is, interestingly enough, used in rocket propulsion fuels.

Some medical mycologists classify *Gyromitra esculenta* as a highly toxic species along with other deadly poisonous mushrooms such as *Amanita phalloides, A. verna, A. virosa* (destroying angel), a few species of the *Cortinarius* genus such as *C. speciosissimus* and *C. orellanus, Galerina autumnalis,* and a few others. Such species "can cause death" even when ingested in small quantities.[3] Small children as well as old, debilitated persons are particularly vulnerable. Fortunately, many of the toxic species are not seen during an early spring mushroom hunt. Yet, not all the *Gyromitras* are to be feared. Such species as *G. gigas,* which grows in the Pacific Northwest, and *G. caroliniana,* which is found in the Southeast and east-central states, are typically classified as edible. Yet, because this is a guide for the novice mushroom hunter, and a novice might not be able to distinguish between the various species, I recommend avoiding the *Gyromitra* genus as a whole.

Other species, such as members of the genus *Helvella,* are usually included in the general category of false morels, and therefore, the same caution is needed with these as with the *Gyromitra* genus. A detailed description of these species is beyond the scope of this book.

Morels, as well as many other edible species of mushrooms, are delectable additions to the menu due to their delicate flavor and texture in side dishes, soups, and sauces. They are a valuable nutritional supplement containing many minerals and some antioxidants. Most mushrooms contain vita-

2. Orson K. Miller, *Mushrooms of North America* (New York: E. P. Dutton, 1979), 327.
3. Joseph R. Dipalma, Hahnemann Medical College, Philadelphia, "Mushroom Poisoning," *Clinical Pharmacology* 23, no. 5 (May 1981).

mins B_1 and B_2 and an appreciable amount of protein. They are fat free, of low caloric content, and simply delicious. There are a thousand ways to use them. In Japan, China, and other Eastern countries they are often used as medicinals, but primarly they are used in the kitchen.

How to Use Morels
in the Kitchen

Morels, in my view and according to most mycophagists (folks who enjoy eating wild mushrooms), are one of the top three species for the table. The other two, the white and black truffles (*Tuber melanosporum* and *T. magnatum*), are both prized, especially by the French and Italians, and *Boletus edulis* (the king bolete, known in Europe as the porcini, cep, or steinpilz) is prized by everyone who has tried it. But morels are great. They have an excellent woodsy flavor and pleasant texture. The flavor of the black morel is a bit more intense, but it is less meaty than the gray and yellow morels. I like them all, though I sometimes prefer one over the other depending on the meal they will accompany.

In the recipes that follow you can use either fresh morels or previously sautéed and frozen mushrooms. You will not notice any difference.

Now for the best part—eating morels. To me, these meals taste better because I have outwitted cunning nature and brought home a basket of wild morels. This is particularly satisfying since buying just a couple of pounds of these beauties would set me back a noticeable fraction of my paycheck. Fresh morels in Michigan sell for up to twenty-five dollars a pound, depending on how plentiful the crop, and one rarely sees fresh morels in stores. The main reason for this is their relatively short shelf life. But the sale of mushrooms is also regulated by the states, and the typical source for the mushrooms is usually an individual trying to earn a few extra dollars. If you buy fresh mushrooms from roadside vendors, you should exercise a bit of caution since you occasionally see a mélange of edible and nonedible varieties. Dried morels do occasionally appear in stores at about three to five dollars an ounce, some coming from as far away as Chile. The quality of all these mushrooms can be highly questionable.

Many mushroom recipes, from very simple dishes to elaborate feasts, have been concocted by famous chefs who devote their skills to haute cuisine. Since the primary purpose of this volume is to help the reader find morels, I have confined this chapter to just a few favorite recipes. As noted earlier, there are several fast and simple ways to prepare morels. Some friends from Indiana and Ohio who come each spring to hunt morels in northern Michigan simply roll fresh whole mushrooms in flour and fry them in bacon grease. While this dish can be easily prepared even over an open campfire, it is not a favorite of my wife and me. The recipes that my wife offers here require a bit more work, yet anybody with fair kitchen skills should be able to follow these recipes and come up with a dish worthy of lavish compliments. Let's slip on an apron and get to some enjoyable and rewarding work!

Chicken Paprika with Morels

3 tablespoons fat of choice (half margarine, half butter)
1 medium-sized onion, chopped
1 tablespoon sweet paprika
Dash of hot paprika (optional)
1 chicken, 2½ to 4 pounds, cut up and dusted with flour, salt, and pepper
1½ cups chicken broth or bouillon
½ pound fresh morels, sliced (halved if smaller)
2 tablespoons flour

½ to ¾ cup sour cream
Salt and pepper to taste

Sauté onions in heated fat until they are wilted. Add paprika and chicken. When chicken is browned on both sides, add broth, cover, and simmer for 30 to 45 minutes until chicken pieces are almost tender. Add mushrooms and simmer 15 minutes longer. Remove chicken pieces to a warm platter. Mix flour into sour cream and carefully stir into sauce. Heat through but do not boil. Pour sauce over chicken and serve over hot pasta, rice, or dumplings. Serves four to five.

Chicken paprika with morels served with Czech dumplings

Fresh Morel Pâté

½ cup butter
1 cup morels, coarsely chopped
½ cup onion, finely minced
2 tablespoons dry sherry or 1 tablespoon sherry and 1 tablespoon chicken broth

2 to 3 ounces cream cheese
1/3 cup fresh parsley, minced
Salt and pepper to taste

Sauté mushrooms, onions, salt, and pepper in butter until mushrooms are tender. Add sherry. In a food processor, process cheese and parsley. Add the mushroom mixture and pulse on and off a few times until the mixture reaches a smooth consistency (but leave some mushrooms in small chunks). Serve at room temperature with crackers or on toast points.

Wild Mushroom and Rice Soup

1/2 and 3/4 cup onions, chopped
2 garlic cloves, minced
2 to 3 tablespoons butter, divided
1 cup packaged wild and white rice mix
2 to 3 cups water
4 cups morels or other mushrooms, sliced
1/2 teaspoon dried rosemary
5 cups chicken stock (large can)
Pinch of fresh rosemary, minced
1/2 to 3/4 cup heavy cream
Salt and pepper to taste

Sauté 1/2 cup of onions and the garlic in 2 tablesppons butter for a few minutes. Add rice mix and sauté for a few more minutes. Add water and simmer in an uncovered pot over low heat for about 30 minutes. Drain any excess water.

Sauté the mushrooms in remaining butter. Add 3/4 cup of onions and dried rosemary and sauté a little longer. Add chicken stock and simmer an additional 15 minutes or until mushrooms and onions are tender. (For a thicker soup, puree a ladleful and return it to the pot.) Add drained rice, cream, and salt and pepper to taste. Simmer until the soup is hot, then sprinkle with fresh rosemary. Serves four to five.

Morel Mousse

This dish is very delicate and is great served alongside a chicken or beef dish that has a nice sauce or gravy.

2 cups morels, sliced
2 or 3 shallots, sliced (or ¼ Vidalia or other sweet onion, chopped)
1½ tablespoons butter
Splash of port wine
Splash of Madeira
½ cup heavy cream
1 tablespoon sour cream
2 eggs
Salt, pepper, and grated nutmeg to taste

Sauté mushrooms and shallots in butter until tender. Add salt, pepper, port, and Madeira. Then flame.

Place the mixture in a food processor and pulse for 5 or 6 seconds. Add cream, sour cream, eggs, nutmeg, and more salt or pepper if desired. Process until fully pureed.

Place the mixture in buttered ½ to ¾ cup molds. Place filled molds on a baking pan, fill the baking pan with hot water to half the height of the molds. Bake in a 325°F oven for 30 minutes.

After removing the molds from the oven, remove from hot water bath and let stand for about 5 minutes. Run a knife around the edges of the molds to loosen the mousse, place a saucer on top of each mold, and flip the contents onto the saucer. Serve with a sauce of your choice. Makes five to six molds.

Mushroom Casserole

1 pound fresh mushrooms (morels, shiitakes, button mush-
    rooms, or a mixture), cut in large pieces
4 tablespoons butter, divided
½ cup onion, chopped
½ cup green pepper, chopped
½ cup celery, chopped
½ cup mayonnaise
¾ teaspoon salt
¼ teaspoon freshly ground pepper
6 slices white bread, cubed
2 eggs
1½ cups milk (or ¾ cup half and half and ¾ cup milk)
10¾ ounce can condensed cream of mushroom soup
¼ cup Parmesan cheese, grated

Sauté the mushrooms with the onions, green peppers, and celery in 2 tablesppons of butter until soft but not brown. Remove from heat. Add mayonnaise, salt, and pepper and mix well.

In a separate skillet sauté bread cubes in the remaining butter over medium-high heat until golden. Place half the bread cubes in the bottom of a 2½ quart casserole dish or a 9 by 13 inch baking dish. Add vegetable mixture and top with remaining bread cubes.

Mix eggs and milk, beating well. Pour over the casserole. Refrigerate for at least 1 hour, preferably overnight. One hour before serving spread mushroom soup evenly over the top. Cover and bake in a 300°F oven for 50 minutes. Remove, sprinkle with Parmesan cheese, then return to oven, uncovered, for 10 minutes. Serves six.

Old-Fashioned Baked Eggs with Mushrooms

1 pound fresh mushrooms, cleaned
7 tablespoons butter, divided
8 eggs, hard-boiled and shelled
2 tablespoons Parmesan cheese, grated
3 tablespoons flour
2 cups milk (or a combination of half and half and milk)
6 slices bacon, diced
1 cup potatoes, diced
¼ cup onion, minced
Salt, pepper, and grated nutmeg to taste

Remove stems from mushrooms. Set caps aside. (Mushroom caps may be sliced in half if desired.) Chop stems finely, sauté in 2 tablespoons butter for 3 minutes. Remove from heat.

Cut hard-boiled eggs in half lengthwise and place yolks and whites in separate bowls. Add to the yolks the sautéed stems together with any drippings, cheese, nutmeg, salt, and pepper. Spoon mixture into the egg white cavities and arrange in a shallow buttered baking dish.

Melt 2 tablespoons butter in a saucepan. Stir in flour. Cook over medium heat, stirring constantly, for 1 minute. Gradually add milk and cook slowly, stirring, until thick and smooth. Gently pour the sauce around the filled egg whites.

Melt remaining 3 tablespoons butter in a skillet and add mushroom caps. Add a little salt and pepper and sauté for 4 minutes. Spoon mushrooms over sauce. Fry bacon pieces until crisp. Sprinkle over mushroom caps.

Fry potatoes in the skillet until tender, adding minced onion. Spoon over bacon. Bake in a 350°F oven for about 20 minutes until hot and bubbly. Serves five.

Stuffed Fennel Boats

This is an exquisite dish worthy of being served in the most exclusive restaurants.

2 large fennel bulbs
1 medium-sized Vidalia or other sweet onion, chopped
2 tablespoons butter
2 chicken breasts, skinned and boned, and cut into pieces
8 ounces or 2½ cups yellow morels, trimmed and chopped
4 tablespoons flour
1¼ cup chicken broth, canned or homemade, heated
3 eggs, hard-boiled and shelled
1 teaspoon Dijon mustard
2 teaspoons dry sherry
Salt and pepper to taste
Fennel greens for garnish

Trim off the base and pull each fennel bulb apart. Arrange the outer layers to make 5 stuffing boats. Finely chop the inner parts of the bulbs and set aside.

Boil the fennel boats in salted water 2 to 3 minutes. Remove from water and allow them to cool. In a skillet, gently sauté chopped fennel bits and onion in butter for 3 to 4 minutes.

Add chicken and morels to the skillet and sauté over medium heat for about 6 minutes, stirring often. Stir in flour. Remove from heat. Gradually add the heated chicken broth making sure the flour is well blended with the broth. Return to heat and simmer until thickened, stirring constantly. Chop one of the eggs into the mixture. Add mustard, sherry, salt, and pepper.

Arrange the fennel boats in a shallow baking dish. Spoon filling into the boats. (There will be stuffing left over.) Cover with aluminum foil and bake for 20 to 25 minutes in a 375°F

Close-up of stuffed fennel boats

oven. Serve on a bed of rice garnished with quartered eggs and fennel sprigs.

Pork Sausage Puff with Wild Mushrooms

1 clove garlic, crushed
2 pinches dried thyme or 1 tablespoon fresh, chopped
4 to 5 cups black morels or other wild mushrooms, cleaned and sliced
4 tablespoons butter
1 cup fresh white bread crumbs (about 2 bread slices pulsed in a food processor)
5 tablespoons fresh parsley, chopped
1 sheet puff pastry (left at room temperature for 30 minutes)
1 to 1½ pounds bulk pork sausage
1 egg, beaten with a pinch of salt
Salt and pepper to taste

Gently sauté garlic, thyme, and morels in butter. The morels will give off some liquid. Continue to sauté until it evaporates, 5 to 6 minutes. Stir in bread crumbs and parsley and season with salt and pepper.

Roll out puff pastry on a floured surface to create a 14 by 10 inch rectangle. Transfer pastry to a large ungreased baking sheet with sides. Remove the casing from the sausage and discard. Chop the sausage into small pieces. Place half the sausage in a strip about 5 inches wide down the middle of the long side of the pastry, leaving at least a 2 inch unfilled border on each side. Cover sausage with mushroom mixture then add another layer of meat.

Make a series of slanting cuts toward the center 1 inch apart on the long sides of pastry, leaving an area 1 to 1½ inches from the filling uncut. Fold top and bottom uncut ends of the pastry over the filling, moisten with beaten egg, then cross the top of the meat with alternate strips of pastry from the cut sides, pinching each 2 strips together at the top.

Brush pastry with egg and bake for 1 hour in a 350°F oven. The sides of the baking sheet will contain any fat that might leak from the puff. Serves five to six.

Morel Cream Puffs

For the puffs:
½ cup milk or water
½ stick (4 tablespoons) unsalted butter, cut into small pieces
½ teaspoon salt
½ cup flour
2 large eggs

For the filling:
1 small onion, chopped
¼ cup raw bacon, diced

Morel cream puffs served with breast of chicken

4 cups morels, chopped
¾ teaspoon salt
1 cup cooked ham, diced
½ cup soft bread crumbs (1 slice of bread pulsed in a food
   processor)

To make the puffs, combine milk (or water), butter, and salt in
a saucepan and bring to a boil over medium heat. Add flour
all at once, stirring vigorously with a wooden spoon. When
mixture no longer clings to the sides of the pan, remove from
heat. Do not overcook! Let mixture cool for about 5 minutes,
stirring occasionally.

   Add eggs, one at a time, beating vigorously with a
wooden spoon. (Be sure mixture is smooth before adding the

second egg.) Beat until smooth, shiny, and stiff. Preheat oven to 400°F with rack at the lowest position.

Drop spoonfuls of dough onto an ungreased baking sheet, leaving space for expansion. There should be about 10 puffs 2 to 3 inches in diameter. You can also use a pastry bag fitted with a plain tip. Bake for 10 minutes on the low rack. Reduce temperature to 350°F and bake for 25 minutes longer or until puffs are firm to the touch. Remove to a cooling rack. With a knife cut a hole in the side of each puff to let out the steam. When cool, slice in half horizontally, remove any uncooked dough, and set aside.

To make the filling, sauté onion and bacon until tender. Add morels and salt. The morels will give off some liquid. Continue to sauté until it evaporates, about 15 minutes. Add ham and bread crumbs and sauté 5 minutes more.

To serve, fill the bottom half of each hollowed-out puff with the morel mixture and place the other half of the puff on top. Serve with a sauce of your choice.

Morel Tart

9-inch piecrust (your own or prepackaged)
2 handfuls of gray or yellow morels, chopped
2 cloves garlic, minced
½ cup Vidalia or other sweet onion, chopped
2 tablespoons butter
¼ cup sherry
3 tablespoons Parmesan cheese
3 tablespoons Gruyère cheese
3 eggs
1 cup half and half
1 teaspoon Dijon mustard

Bake the piecrust at 400°F for 9 to 12 minutes until golden brown. Do not prick the bottom. Remove the piecrust and let it cool, but leave the oven on. Sauté mushrooms, garlic, and onion in melted butter. Cook until tender. Add sherry and sauté until it evaporates. Spread the mixture into the baked piecrust. Sprinkle with 2 tablespoons Parmesan and 2 tablespoons Gruyère cheese. Beat together eggs, half and half, and mustard. Place the filled crust on a cookie sheet with sides and carefully pour the egg mixture into it. Sprinkle remaining cheese on top and bake for 20 to 25 minutes. Cool the tart for 8 to 10 minutes before cutting.

Chicken Aspen

1 pound morels (preferably gray or yellow), cleaned and
   chopped
½ cup onion, minced
4 tablespoons butter, divided
½ cup plus 2 or 3 tablespoons sherry or Madeira
2 to 3 tablespoons flour
1 to 1½ cups chicken stock
¾ to 1 cup heavy cream
4 boneless, skinless chicken breasts, dusted with flour, salt,
   and pepper

Sauté mushrooms and onions in 2 tablespoons butter for a few minutes. Add sherry and continue to sauté until it has almost evaporated. Add flour and stir to make a thick roux. Add chicken stock and stir until the sauce is medium thick. Add cream and heat for a few more minutes until the sauce is as thick as you wish.

Sauté chicken breasts in butter until tender, add additional 2 or 3 tablespoons of sherry or Madeira to skillet and stir until it evaporates. Turn over onto a heated serving platter. Cover the chicken with sauce. Serve with pasta, dumplings, or cooked rice made with peas. Serves four.

Morel-Filled Omelets

For the filling:
2 tablespoons butter
½ cup onion, finely chopped
1 pound morels, chopped
1 tablespoon finely chopped parsley
1 tablespoon (or less) flour
4 tablespoons chicken stock or cream
Salt and pepper to taste

For the omelets:
12 eggs
6 tablespoons milk
3 tablespoons butter (or a little more)
Salt
Parsley sprigs and tomato segments for garnish (optional)

To make the filling, melt butter in a skillet and sauté the onions, morels, parsley, and salt until the onions and mushrooms are tender. The morels will give off some liquid. Continue to cook until it evaporates. Mix in flour and sauté a bit more. Add the chicken stock or cream and cook the sauce gently until it thickens, adding more stock or cream if it becomes too thick. Place skillet in a warm oven.

To prepare the eggs, combine eggs, milk, and salt in a large bowl and beat until well blended.

To make the omelets, remove the filling from the oven.

Melt ½ tablespoon butter over high heat in an 8 inch omelet pan or small skillet. When the butter is hot, add ½ cup of the egg mixture, keeping the heat on high. Lift up the edges of the egg mixture to allow any uncooked portions to flow underneath. Repeat several times. Do not overcook.

When the omelet is still slightly moist on top, place one-sixth of the filling on half of the omelet and fold the other half over the top. Slip the omelet out of the pan onto a warm plate. Continue with the rest of the omelets.

Garnish with parsley and tomato segments if desired. Serves six.

Scallops with Morels and White Sauce

For the sauce:
4 tablespoons butter
½ cup flour
2 cups milk or half and half
Salt and white pepper to taste
Dash of grated nutmeg

For the scallops:
6 to 8 sea scallops
5 tablespoons butter, divided
2 shallots, finely chopped (or 2 slices of Vidalia or other
    sweet onion)
2 garlic cloves, finely chopped
1 teaspoon fresh thyme, finely chopped, or 1 large pinch of
    dried
½ pound morels, stems removed, coarsely chopped
2 slices of Italian prosciutto or ham, chopped
¼ cup dry sherry
3 tablespoons Parmesan cheese, finely grated
Salt and pepper to taste

To prepare the white sauce, melt butter in a skillet and add flour. Cook, stirring constantly, over low heat for a few minutes or until butter and flour are combined. Add milk or half and half and bring to a boil, whisking to keep it smooth. Boil until sauce becomes quite thick. Add salt, pepper, and nutmeg.

To prepare the scallops, wash them under cold water and set aside.

To prepare the morels, in a skillet melt 3 or 4 tablespoons of butter, add shallots and garlic, and cook slowly over low heat. Add thyme, morels, and prosciutto. Season with salt and pepper and sauté until mushrooms are tender. Add sherry and continue to sauté until it evaporates.

To complete the dish, preheat oven to 400°F. Butter 4 to 6 (depending on size) individual gratin dishes or scallop shells. Chop scallops coarsely and place in shells. Stir morel mixture into white sauce and adjust the seasonings if necessary. Spoon sauce over scallops. Sprinkle with cheese and place on a large cookie sheet. Bake for 10 to 15 minutes and serve immediately. Serves four to six.

Morel Strata with Cheese and Sausage

This nice breakfast casserole can be assembled the night before and baked in the morning. It is also ideal for brunch. It can be baked after a couple of hours of refrigeration if necessary.

1 to 2 pounds bulk sausage
2 large handfuls morels, stems removed, roughly chopped
½ to ¾ cup chopped Vidalia or other sweet onion
½ loaf Italian bread, cubed, divided
¾ pound Swiss or other melting cheese, shredded (about 3
    cups), divided
2½ cups milk (or a combination of half and half and milk)
5 or 6 eggs, depending on size
Salt and pepper to taste

Sauté sausage until thoroughly cooked, breaking it into pieces with a wooden spoon as it cooks. Remove all but a few spoonfuls of fat, add morels and onions, and cook until juices evaporate. Set aside. In a large greased baking dish place half the bread cubes. Add sausage mixture and 2 cups of cheese. Place the rest of the bread cubes on top and sprinkle with remaining cheese. Whisk together milk, eggs, salt, and pepper. Slowly pour egg mixture over the strata until it appears to be well soaked to the top, pressing down occasionally. Cover and refrigerate for at least 2 hours or overnight. Bake in a 350°F oven for 40 to 50 minutes or until puffed. The strata is done when a wooden skewer inserted in the center comes out clean.

Mushroom Hunters' Etiquette

Most of us have probably heard reports of the behavior of some professional mushroom pickers on the West Coast—people who gather wild mushrooms and sell them on the commercial market. There have allegedly been incidents of violent engagements between competing pickers, some reaching the level of shooting. While some mushroom hunters consider their competitors adversaries and rivals, since they are competing for a limited harvest, most morel hunters realize that we need to exercise civility and abide by certain rules of etiquette in our pursuit of the quarry.

First of all, we need to respect private property. There is always a tract of public land open to the wild mushroom gatherer. Most private lands are posted along the main road, and while it is easy to stray unintentionally onto private property in areas where private tracts are interwoven with public land, we can minimize such incidents by acquiring and studying a large-scale map that defines the boundaries of the area's public land. A mushroom hunter can also try to identify the owner of a property and seek permission to hunt on his or her land. Most state parks, state forests, and even national forests are open to the mushroom hunter (although some national forests in heavily hunted areas require a permit and limit the quantity of picked mushrooms). National parks prohibit the picking of flowers and fungi alike.

Mushroom hunters should also avoid invading an area

occupied by another hunter actively engaged in gathering the fruits of the forest. There is no definite rule as to the distance we must keep between ourselves and our fellow mushroomers, and we may accidentally pass through an area in which someone else is searching; however, we must never intentionally invade a territory because we see that our competitor has struck gold.

Being ecologically responsible also involves an effort to protect the surrounding plant life, to never trample on wildflowers, and to protect young shrubs and bushes.

While most of us enjoy the salutary benefits of the exercise involved in mushroom hunting, there are some that call upon the speed of motorized all-terrain vehicles (ATVs) to give themselves a competitive edge. I have no objection to the speed because the forest's topography will always limit a motorized vehicle's value, but I do object to the noise created by these revved-up machines. The spring forest is a heavenly and relaxing place that reflects the peace and beauty of nature—full of the scents of wild leeks and spring flowers, quiet except for the song of birds. While looking for mushrooms, I enjoy this solitude and tranquility; it is an escape from the city, from its polluted air and the noise of automobiles, trains, and machinery. The horrible racket of a colony of ATVs breaks this silence and returns me to the place from which I have temporarily escaped. I personally believe that such motorized vehicles ought to be prohibited in state and national forests, but until they are we can only appeal to their owners to respect the rights of others. We can also let them know that they are much more likely to find mushrooms using their own two feet.

I shouldn't have to mention that beer cans, bottles, and other waste products should be left in the garbage at home and not disposed of in the forest. If one is willing to tolerate garbage in his or her own backyard, so be it! But please don't defile the beauty of nature. Public lands belong to everyone.

A garden of spring trilliums

When canoeing in the Boundary Waters Canoe Area or at Quetico, I pack out every item that isn't biodegradable. If people were to leave their garbage scattered around the campground, it would soon wreck the experience for everyone. So whatever you bring in, pack out! If you brought it in full, it shouldn't be a problem to carry it back empty. Don't ask others to clean up after you!

A final irritant to the mushroom hunter is the logging industry. State and federal governments sell the rights to take timber from public lands to private logging companies. Although I do not oppose a limited and orderly harvest of timber, it is unconscionable for officials of the U.S. Department of Agriculture (USDA) and state departments of natural resources to allow loggers to ravage a forest—leaving behind a tangle of branches, ruts made by tractors and bulldozers, and general disfigurement. The contracting logging company ought to be required to remove all garbage so that the forest is usable after the plunder. I personally think that the contract, which is often of questionable profit to the government (though not necessarily to government officials), should require that the logger be responsible for the reforestation of the area. But that might be too much to expect.

Etiquette is not law. It is behavior that should have been taught to us by our parents. By practicing it, we can make the outdoors more enjoyable for all.

Wouldn't It Be Easier to Pick Them in Our Backyards?

Mushroom lovers have long been able to purchase kits and grow mushrooms in their basements. Initially, only a white mushroom (*Agaricus bisporus*), the so-called meadow mushroom or field mushroom, was available. It was usually supplied in a plastic sack filled with soil mixed with horse manure and inoculated with the mushroom spawn. Placed in a cool (50 to 60°F) room and watered, these kits would soon produce several flushes of mushrooms. Gradually, the menu was expanded to include various other mushrooms—oyster mushrooms (*Pleurotus ostreatus*), blewits (*Clitocybe nuda*), king stropharia (*Stropharia rugosoannulata*), and others. In each of these cases, mushroom cultivation was limited to saprophytic varieties—mushrooms that thrive on decomposing organic plant material or animal excrement. To cultivate fungi that grow on trees, it is necessary to purchase spore-impregnated plugs that are inserted into logs of an appropriate tree and sealed with wax. In a year or two, they produce a crop that keeps returning until the log is digested by the fungi. I used this process and inoculated about a dozen oak logs with shiitake (*Lentinula edodes*) spores and have been obtaining two or three flushes of mushrooms every year since. But it is much more difficult to grow fungi such as morels, which live in a symbiotic relationship with trees.

Cultivating morels at home was a tough nut to crack. As Thomas J. Volk of the USDA Forest Products Laboratory in

Madison, Wisconsin, explained, "The apparent lack of identifiable consistent conditions that lead to wild morel fruiting has been a major deterrent in establishing protocols for artificial morel cultivation."[1] But a number of mycologists have worked on the problem, and about twenty-five years ago Ronald Ower of San Francisco came up with a process for growing morels indoors. The Michigan-based company Neogen then undertook a joint venture with Michigan State University and, with the cooperation of Mr. Ower, developed a commercial process for growing morels. Today there are several commercial enterprises that sell morel kits in which mushrooms grow in a mixture composed of deciduous tree bark and leaf compost. The cultivation process is complicated; one has to adhere rigorously to the detailed steps and must have the required equipment to control all variables in the prescribed manner. A commercial grower may be able to abide by this strict process, but an individual grower requires the right weather and some luck in order to succeed. But we are gradually reaching the point where a dedicated individual with an available plot of land will be able to grow morels in his or her own backyard.

While I think that growing mushrooms at home is interesting and enjoyable, I still relish the excitement of the hunt, the fresh air, and the thrill of the contest with nature as I try to discover the hiding places of the wily morel.

---

1. Thomas J. Volk, "Understanding the Morel Life Cycle: Key to Cultivation," *McIlvainea* 10, no. 1 (1991): 76. *McIlvainea: Journal of American Amateur Mycology* is published by the North American Mycological Association.

Selected Readings

Dickinson, Colin, and John Lucas. *The Encyclopedia of Mushrooms.* New York: G. P. Putnam, 1979.

Graham, Verne O. *Mushrooms of the Great Lakes Region.* New York: Dover, 1970.

Kuo, Michael. *Morels.* Ann Arbor: University of Michigan Press, 2005.

Læssøe, Thomas, Anna Del Conte, and Gary Lincoff. *The Mushroom Book.* New York: DK Publishing, 1996.

Lincoff, Gary. *The Audubon Society Field Guide to North American Mushrooms.* New York: Alfred A. Knopf, 1981.

Lincoff, Gary. *Simon and Schuster's Guide to Mushrooms.* New York: Fireside, 1982.

Miller, Orson K., Jr. *Mushrooms of North America.* New York: E. P. Dutton, 1979.

Phillips, Roger. *Mushrooms of North America.* Boston: Little, Brown, 1991.

Rinaldi, Augusto, and Vassili Tyndalo. *The Complete Book of Mushrooms.* New York: Crown, 1974.

Smith, Alexander, and Nancy Smith Weber. *The Mushroom Hunter's Field Guide.* Ann Arbor: University of Michigan Press, 1980.

Weber, Nancy Smith. *A Morel Hunter's Companion.* Holt, MI: Thunder Bay Press, 1995.

Other Sources of Information about Mushrooms

Harris, Bob. *Growing Wild Mushrooms.* Berkeley: Wingbow Press, 2003.
McIlvainea: Journal of American Amateur Mycology. Published by the North American Mycological Association.
Wikipedia, http://en.wikipedia.org/wiki/Mushroom
Mushroom Expert, http://www.mushroomexpert.com

Mushroom-Growing Kits

Fungi Perfecti, http://www.fungi.com

Mushroom Products and Fresh and Dried Mushrooms

Creekside Mushrooms, http://www.creeksidemushrooms.com
Gourmet Mushrooms and Mushroom Products, http://www.gmushrooms.com
Oregon Mushrooms, http://www.oregonmushrooms.com
Pacific Mushrooms, http://www.pacificmushrooms.com
Dried Mushrooms, Wild Mushrooms, http://www.dried-mushrooms.us

Mushroom Recipes

Southern Food, http://www.southernfood.about.com/

Checklist of Shroomers' Implements

☐ Walking stick (light and sturdy)

☐ Mosquito repellent (preferably at least 40 percent DEET)

☐ Compass or GPS

☐ Knife

☐ Canvas bag, basket, or other suitable container for mushrooms

☐ Raincoat

☐ Light, waterproof boots with ridged soles

☐ Whistle

☐ Walkie-talkie (if hunting with a partner or partners)

☐ Map indicating boundaries of public land

☐ Drinking water

☐ Notebook and pencil

☐ Premoistened towelettes

Morel Hunters' Timetable

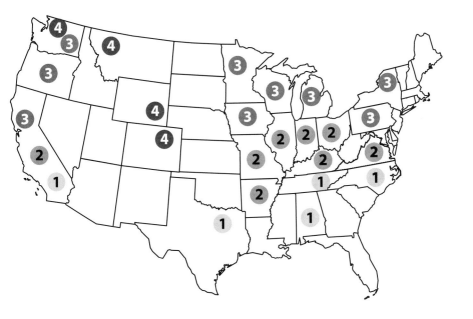

Zone ❶ March 15–April 15
Zone ❷ April 10–May 10
Zone ❸ May 10–May 31
Zone ❹ May 15 and later, depending on elevation

Text design by Mary H. Sexton
Typesetting by Delmastype, Ann Arbor, Michigan

Font: Janson Text
Designed by the Hungarian Nicholas Kis in about 1690, the
model for Janson Text was mistakenly attributed to the Dutch
printer Anton Janson. Kis' original matrices were found in
Germany and acquired by the Stempel foundry in 1919. Its
strong design and clear stroke contrast combine to create text
that is both elegant and easy to read.
—courtesy www.adobe.com